D0908912

Halloween Crafts

Halloween Crafts

★ A Holiday Craft Book ★

★ Judith Hoffman Corwin ★

FRANKLIN WATTS

New York ★ Chicago ★ London ★ Toronto ★ Sydney

★ **Also by Judith Hoffman Corwin** ★

African Crafts
Asian Crafts
Latin American and Caribbean Crafts

Colonial American Crafts: The Home
Colonial American Crafts: The School
Colonial American Crafts: The Village

Easter Crafts
Kwanzaa Crafts
Thanksgiving Crafts
Valentine Crafts

Papercrafts

Forthcoming Books

Christmas Crafts
Hanukkah Crafts

★ **For Jules Arthur and Oliver Jamie** ★

Library of Congress Cataloging-in-Publication Data

Corwin, Judith Hoffman.
    Halloween crafts / Judith Hoffman Corwin.
      p.   cm. — (Holiday crafts)
    Includes index.
    ISBN 0-531-11148-2
    1. Halloween decorations—Juvenile literature.   2. Handicraft—
Juvenile literature.   3. Halloween cookery—Juvenile literature.
[1. Halloween decorations.   2. Handicraft.   3. Halloween cookery.]
I. Title.   II. Series: Corwin, Judith Hoffman.   Holiday crafts.
TT900.H32C66   1995
745.594′1—dc20

                      93-6367
                      CIP   AC

Contents

About Halloween

Everyone looks forward to Halloween because of all the fun of dressing up as something special—a monster, witch, ballerina, bat, or ghost—and going with friends from door to door to collect candy and other treats. It's a time for parties and pumpkins carved as jack-o'-lanterns put into windows to light trick-or-treaters' paths. Sometimes you can collect enough candy to last for weeks! Just be careful to eat only wrapped candy that has been checked by an adult.

Halloween is a very old holiday. It was started by the Celts, a group of people who lived in Scotland and Ireland in ancient times. The Celts held a special festival to honor Samhain, the god of the dead, on what was their New Year's Eve—October 31 on our calendar. The souls of the dead were believed to return to visit their homes at this time. Huge bonfires were lit to scare away any evil spirits that might harm the people or their herds of cattle and sheep returning from the pastures where they had grazed all summer.

This Celtic festival was combined with another celebration during the Middle Ages in Scotland and Ireland. All Hallows—a feast in honor of all the Christian saints—was celebrated on November 1. People believed that on All Hallows' Eve witches, sometimes in the form of black cats, flew about, and ghosts, demons, and goblins were thought to roam the land. All Hallows' Eve was also a time for fortune-telling—who would marry whom, how long they would live, and if they would be lucky. It was a time, too, for games like bobbing for apples, which we play to this day. The Irish believed that "the little people" played pranks on Halloween, and so mischief-making became part of the festivities. In time, All Hallows' Eve became "Halloween." About 150 years ago, at a time when many Scotch and Irish people emigrated to the United States, the Halloween tradition was brought along.

A favorite symbol of Halloween is the jack-o'-lantern. A hollowed-out turnip was used in Scotland to make a lantern, but the pumpkin is native to the United States and is used here. A Halloween tradition that is popular here is for trick-or-treaters to collect money for UNICEF, the United Nations International Children's Emergency Fund. Every Halloween, millions of children in the United States help others around the world who are less fortunate. ★

TRICK OR TREAT

Let's Get Started

This book will help you learn about the Halloween holiday, its legends, and its history. Here are ideas for making decorations, greeting cards, presents, gift wrappings, and wonderful things to eat. You will be able to make everything yourself, using everyday household supplies and objects. Use your imagination and you will be surprised at what you can create. The treasures that you make will add color and excitement to your holiday celebrations. Sometimes you will need an adult to help with a few steps in a project.

Directions for some of the projects include patterns for you to use to make a copy of what is shown. You don't want to cut up this book, so copy the pattern with tracing paper. Begin by placing a piece of tracing paper over the pattern in the book. Using a pencil with a soft lead, trace the outline of the pattern. Turn the paper over and rub all over the pattern with the pencil. Turn it over again, and tape or hold it down carefully on the paper or fabric you have chosen to work with. Draw over your original lines, pressing hard on the pencil. Lift the tracing-paper pattern and you are ready to go on with the other instructions for your project.★

Ten Little Ghosts★

There are ten ghosts in the bathroom,
There are nine ghosts down the hall,
There are eight ghosts near the closet,
There are seven ghosts under the sofa,
There are six ghosts on the mantel,
There are five ghosts in the kitchen,
There are four ghosts at the window,
There are three ghosts out in the garden,
Where two other ghosts are having tea,
And there's one ghost behind a tree . . .
and that's the one,
that's after *me!*

Saved★

I saw a ghost
    Behind the stairs
He wore a long sheet
    Or underwear!
He knew that I would have
    a scare
If he reached forward and
    pulled my hair.
He did . . .
    I jumped and took
a fall.
    I saw his shadow creep
through the wall.
    As he vanished I laughed
and cried
    until my mother was
by my side.

Haunted Halloween Poems

Here are three original Halloween poems and, on the next page, some poems that were written a long time ago. They should put you in a Halloween mood. Read all the poems and the list of Halloween words and phrases. Now you're ready to start writing your own poem. Take a pencil and paper and write down your ideas and rhymes. Think about all the things that remind you of Halloween and what fun it is to go out trick-or-treating.

Witch of Weobley★

The wicked witch of Weobley Wood,
was always up to no good.
She did whatever she could
to create mischief in the wood.

Ghoulies and Beasties★

From Ghoulies and Ghosties,
And long-leggity Beasties,
And all things that go bump
in the night,
Good Lord deliver us.

Old Cornish litany

A Skeleton Once in Khartoum★

A skeleton once in Khartoum
Asked a spirit up into his room;
They spent the whole night
In the eeriest fight
As to which should be frightened of whom.

Author unknown

The Kilkenny Cats★

There wanst was two cats at Kilkenny,
Each thought there was one cat too many,
So they quarrel'd and fit,
They scratch'd and bit,
Till, excepting their nails,
And the tips of their tails,
Instead of two cats, there warnt any.

Author unknown

Little Jack Pumpkin Face★

Little Jack Pumpkin Face
Lived on a vine,
Little Jack Pumpkin Face
Thought it was fine.
First he was small and green,
Then big and yellow,
Little Jack Pumpkin Face
Is a fine fellow.

A country song

★Words and Phrases for Halloween Poems★

abracadabra
darkest night
shadowy walls
jack-o'-lanterns
black cats
ghostly shapes
pumpkins
spiderwebs
witchcraft
dragons
slinky
scary things
ghoulish
screeching owls
cobwebs
midnight
bogus-boo
phantoms
werewolves
hocus-pocus
caldron-hot
toadstool
broomstick
witches' brew
pumpkin patch
icky, sticky
witch's spell
goblin's goo
glowing eyes
horror
ghostly moans
strange voices in the
    night

quiver and quake
shiver and shake
hooting and howling
haunted houses
lurking spooks
fearsome fright
long-legged beasties
ghoulies and
    ghosties
sulky witch
gnomes and
    leprechauns
invisible spirits
ghosts
demons and devils
monsters and
    witches
vampire bats
zombie
full moon
scarecrow

October night
autumn moon
graveyard antics
flying witches
vultures
snakes
creepy, crawly things
shadows
chilling, thrilling
spooky
evil creatures of the
    night
starry night
rustling leaves
musty smells
skeletons and bones

13

Creatures and Crawly Things

Here are lots of creatures, crawly things, and monster designs for you to use on Halloween party invitations, cards, stationery, wrapping paper, T-shirts, and wall and window decorations.

HERE'S WHAT YOU WILL NEED★

pencil
tracing paper, carbon paper
oaktag or white paper (8½″ × 11″)
tape, scissors, hole punch, string
black fine-line marker
colored felt-tip markers

HERE'S HOW TO DO IT★

1. Trace the design you want to use onto tracing paper.

2. To make stationery, use an 8½″ × 11″ piece of white paper. Place a piece of carbon paper on the paper and tape it down gently. Now tape the traced design on top of the carbon paper.

3. Trace one monster design on the upper left corner and write a message around it. Or fill the page with monsters and leave a small space at the bottom for a message.

4. For a Halloween card, fold the white paper in half. Tape the carbon paper onto the paper. Tape the traced design on top. Put one or more monsters on the front of the card.

5. To make a party invitation, tape the carbon paper and the traced design onto the oaktag. Cut around the outside edge of the design. Then punch a hole at the top of the card and pull a string about 8″ long through it. The reverse side of the card can be used for your message. Wall and window decorations can be made the same way, using oaktag. Decorate both sides of the oaktag for the window decorations.

6. Draw over the designs firmly with a pencil. Then remove the tracing paper and carbon paper. Now draw over the outline of the design with a fine-line marker. Color in the rest of the design with the markers. ★

Hendrick the Halloween Cat

This spooky little creature has glowing eyes, white whiskers and nose. This will make a delightful Halloween card or party invitation.

HERE'S WHAT YOU WILL NEED★

(These supplies will make 1 invitation)

1 piece of white paper, 8½″ × 11″
5″ square of black oaktag, or other thin cardboard
pencil
tracing paper
scrap of white paper
glue
tape

HERE'S HOW TO DO IT★

1. Fold the piece of white paper in half along the 11″ side. Now the folded paper is 8½″ × 5½″. Open this up, and that is where you will glue the cat later.

2. Now take the 5″ square of black oaktag and, following the directions given on page 9, trace the cat design on it.

3. Take the scrap of white paper and cut out the cat's eyes, whiskers, and nose. Glue in place, as shown in the illustration. Now tape the cat to the inside center fold of the folded paper, as shown. On the outside of the card write "Happy Halloween." Inside the card write a party invitation or a Halloween message.★

Trick-or-Treat Bags

Here's a quick way to change an ordinary shopping bag into a special Halloween trick-or-treat bag to carry home your goodies. Just glue one of these cut-paper designs onto a solid-color shopping bag and you're all set. There are five designs to choose from: a jack-o'-lantern, owl, witch, spooky cat, or a devil in the moonlight.

HERE'S WHAT YOU WILL NEED★

pencil
tracing paper
scissors
tape
black construction paper
solid-color shopping bag
glue

HERE'S HOW TO DO IT★

1. Select the pattern you like.

2. Trace the pattern from the book and then cut out the tracing. Tape your pattern onto the black construction paper.

3. Cut out the construction paper along the pattern lines. Remove the pattern.

4. Checking the illustration, center the design on your shopping bag, and glue it in place.★

Joplin Jack-O'-Lantern

A glowing jack-o'-lantern is a very important part of the Halloween celebration. His shiny face marks a friendly window or doorstep. They are fun to carve and it's easy to make very different-looking faces. Here's a smiling face, a scary face, a frowning face, and a face with a mouth full of teeth!

HERE'S WHAT YOU WILL NEED★

pumpkin
paper towels
pencil
knife
spoon
empty tin can
candle

HERE'S HOW TO DO IT★

1. **Ask an adult to help you with the knife and candle in this project.** Wipe the pumpkin with a damp paper towel so that it is clean and shiny. Decide which face you are going to use and then draw it on your pumpkin with a pencil, checking the illustration. Be sure to leave room at the top of the pumpkin for a lid.

2. Cut off the top of the pumpkin to make a lid. Remove the lid and then scrape and remove the seeds from the inside of the pumpkin. Now you can carve out the features with a knife.

3. Wash and then thoroughly dry an empty tuna fish or other small tin can. This will be a candle holder. Melt the bottom of the candle slightly and then stand it in the tin, pressing down so that it sticks. Place the candle in its holder inside the pumpkin and light it. Replace the pumpkin lid. Now Joplin Jack-O'-Lantern is ready to work Halloween magic.★

Tissue Paper Ghosts

You can make these little ghosts with white tissue paper or plain white cloth. The head is stuffed with cotton balls and there is a bright orange ribbon tied around the neck.

HERE'S WHAT YOU WILL NEED★

(This makes one ghost)

5 cotton balls
10″ square of white tissue paper or cloth
6″ length of orange ribbon or string
black felt-tip marker

HERE'S HOW TO DO IT★

1. To make the ghost's head place the 5 cotton balls in the center of the square of tissue paper or cloth. Form the head around the cotton balls. Tie with the ribbon under the head. Draw on the eyes and mouth with the marker, as shown in the illustration.

2. If you have lollipops to give out for Halloween you can use them to make your ghosts. Just put the tissue paper over the lollipop to make the head and tie the ribbon under it. Now draw on the ghost's face.★

30

A Dozen Demons

These demons float with the slightest breeze. They look great dancing in a window of your classroom or home. You can make as many as you like. A dozen dancing in a window are a good start.

HERE'S WHAT YOU WILL NEED★

pencil
12 sheets of typing paper (8½″ × 11″)
scissors
black felt-tip marker
12 paper clips
glue
string the length of the window where
   the demons are to hang
tape

HERE'S HOW TO DO IT★

1. With the pencil, copy the demon design onto a piece of paper. It's simple, so just draw it freehand. Now take three more sheets of paper and put them underneath your drawing. Hold all four sheets of paper together and cut out the demon design. Take one of the cut-out demons and use that as a pattern to cut out three more. Repeat until you have 12 demons.

2. With the marker, draw in each demon's eyes and mouth. Push one wire end of a paper clip through the top of each one's head, as shown in the illustration. This will make a hook for stringing up the demon. Put a tiny drop of glue around the hole the paper clip made. This will keep the paper from ripping. Repeat for all the demons.

3. Arrange the demons as you like on the string and tape the string to the window. Your dozen demons are now ready to fly.★

Menacing Monster Mask

This fierce monster mask is fun to wear with your Spidery T-Shirt and with a few of the Gory "Scars" painted on your hands!

HERE'S WHAT YOU WILL NEED★

pencil
tracing paper
carbon paper
oaktag
tape
scissors
black, green, and red markers
hole punch
string

HERE'S HOW TO DO IT★

1. Using a pencil, trace the design for the mask on tracing paper.

2. Place a sheet of carbon paper over the oaktag, place the traced design on top. Gently tape the top and bottom of the three papers (tracing paper, carbon paper, oaktag) onto your work surface. This will prevent the papers from sliding around. Draw over the traced design with a pencil, making sure to press firmly. When you lift off the tracing and carbon papers you will have a copy of the design on the oaktag.

3. Cut out the mask from the oaktag. Cut out two circles for eyes.

4. Draw over all the lines on the mask with the black marker. Color in some of the design with the green marker. Color in the eyebrows with the green marker. Now use a red marker to color in the mouth.

5. Make a hole at each side with the hole punch. Attach a string to each hole, so that you can tie the mask around your head.★

Vernon and Vera Makeup

Vernon and Vera are typical monsters with ghostly pale complexions. Here's how to make yourself look that way in a flash. Both Vernon and Vera wear this super makeup with the Black Magic Cape and Spidery T-Shirt.

HERE'S WHAT YOU WILL NEED★

hand lotion
cotton balls
cornstarch
dark eyebrow pencil
brown, gray, green, or purple eye shadow
red lipstick

HERE'S HOW TO DO IT★

1. Begin by spreading a thin layer of hand lotion all over your face, being careful to avoid your eyes. Then with a cotton ball pat on some cornstarch.

2. Ask permission to use someone's makeup, and draw outlines around your eyes and mouth with a dark eyebrow pencil. Now put on some eye shadow and then some red lipstick.★

Zombie Hands

Zombie Hands come reaching out of the darkest night to add a ghostly touch to your Halloween celebration. You can wear these horrible things or just leave them lying around the house.

HERE'S WHAT YOU WILL NEED★

newspaper, 1 sheet
loose-fitting rubber gloves
black felt-tip marker
strips of gauze bandage, about 1″ wide
glue, red paint, talcum powder

HERE'S HOW TO DO IT★

1. Rip the newspaper into strips and loosely stuff some into the gloves. This will make it easier to work with them.

2. With the black marker, color the fingernails to make them stand out. Beginning with the fingers, wrap the gauze strips around the entire glove until it is completely covered. Glue the gauze down (check the illustration) as you work.

3. Dribble some red paint on your Zombie Hands for a final horrible touch. When the glue and paint are dry, remove the newspaper from the inside of the gloves. Sprinkle some talcum powder inside the gloves to make them easier to pull on and off. Have fun with these Zombie Hands. You can make one hand and wear it, and keep your other hand hidden under your costume, or you can make two hands. You can leave them on a table or chair, or even on your bed to give someone a fright.★

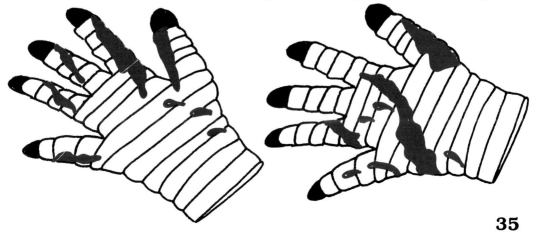

"Frankenstern's" Blood

It's fun to mix up a batch of this. You can apply it to yourself, along with the Gory Scars, or just leave it looking ghoulish in the jar.

HERE'S WHAT YOU WILL NEED★

1 cup corn syrup
empty jar (from jam or peanut butter)
teaspoon
red, yellow, and blue poster paint
red felt-tip marker
3″ square of white paper, tape

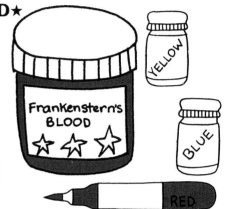

HERE'S HOW TO DO IT★

1. Put the corn syrup into the jar. Add 1 teaspoon of red poster paint and a few drops of yellow and blue paint. Experiment until you get a good, rich color. Mix well.

2. With the red marker, write "Frankenstern's Blood" on the white paper and tape it to the jar for an instant monster's delight!★

Frightful Fangs

These plastic wonders look quite real. Try wearing Vernon or Vera Makeup with a Zombie Hand and the Bat Cape and you are certain to scare a few friendly ghosts.

HERE'S WHAT YOU WILL NEED★

Styrofoam cup, pencil, scissors

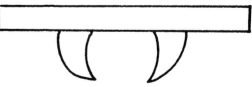

HERE'S HOW TO DO IT★

1. Make sure that the cup is clean before you use it. Use a piece that has a curve so that it can easily be held in your mouth by the upper lip. The top part around the rim is an excellent piece.

2. Checking the illustration, draw the shape onto the Styrofoam with a pencil. Cut it out and then put it into your mouth.★

Gory Scars Galore

With just a few quick brushstrokes . . . *Presto!*, "real" scars. You might want to add a few drops of "Frankenstern's" blood, or carry along the jar of it when you go trick-or-treating.

HERE'S WHAT YOU WILL NEED★

cotton balls
red, purple, and black poster paints
paintbrush

HERE'S HOW TO DO IT★

1.   Using a cotton ball, rub a small amount of purple paint on your cheek or forehead, or wherever you want to make your scar. This will look like a bruise. Let the paint dry.

2.   With either black or red paint draw a long line on the bruise. Make short lines, for stitches, across the long line.

3.   Another Halloween trick is to take a small white box and make a hole in the bottom so that one of your fingers can fit through it. Now surround the hole with some cotton balls. Put your finger (the index finger works best) through the hole. Paint some Gory Scars on it and maybe even a little of "Frankenstern's" blood.★

Black Magic Cape

This cape is very easy to make and can be used for different Halloween costumes. You can wear it with the Bat Mask, the Menacing Monster Mask, the Spidery T-Shirt, a witch's hat, and the Zombie Hands. It's fun to create your own mix-and-match costumes.

HERE'S WHAT YOU WILL NEED★

light-colored crayon or chalk
1 square yard of black felt (You can also use any solid
　color felt or other fabric, or even an old sheet)
scissors
2 pieces of black ribbon, 12″ long
needle, black thread, or stapler

HERE'S HOW TO DO IT★

1.　Draw the outline of the cape on the fabric, using the illustration as a guide.

2.　Cut along the lines you have drawn on the felt.

3.　To make a tie at the front of the cape, sew or staple the 12″ piece of ribbon, as shown in the illustration. Now you will be able to tie the finished cape around you.★

Spidery T-Shirt

This spider in a web is a funny design to draw on a T-shirt. It looks great under the Black Magic Cape, or with the Bat Mask.

HERE'S WHAT YOU WILL NEED★

pencil
tracing paper
white T-shirt, cardboard, carbon paper, tape
permanent black and red felt-tip markers

HERE'S HOW TO DO IT★

1. Trace the spider design, using the tracing paper.

2. Place the T-shirt on the work surface so that the shirt is perfectly flat. The front should face up. Slip a piece of cardboard into the shirt. This will prevent the marker ink from staining the back of the shirt.

3. Place a piece of carbon paper on top of the T-shirt and tape it down. Now tape the traced spiderweb design on top of the carbon paper. Check the illustration for placement.

4. Draw over the design firmly with a pencil. Then remove the tracing paper and carbon paper from the T-shirt, leaving the cardboard in place. Now draw over the design with the black marker. Color the spider's eyes red, and color in the rest of the spider in black.★

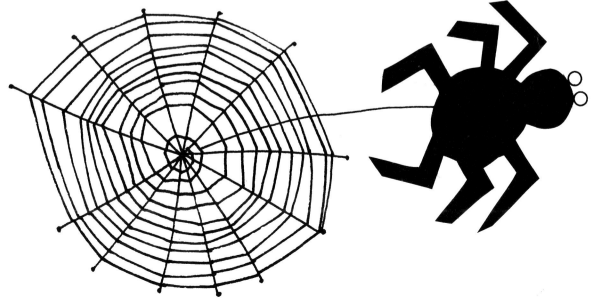

Bat Costume

A black plastic garbage bag makes a terrific bat costume. You can be covered up from the shoulders down, and make a Bat Mask for your head. (Be careful to never have the plastic cover your face.) The wings can be easily made by following the illustrations. In just a few minutes you will be able to cut out your costume.

HERE'S WHAT YOU WILL NEED★

1 black plastic garbage bag
white crayon or chalk
scissors
8½″ × 11″ piece of black construction paper
hole punch
12″ of string, cut in half

HERE'S HOW TO DO IT★

1. On a flat working surface, smooth out the plastic bag. Using the white crayon, sketch the outline of the bat wings onto the plastic bag, as shown in the illustration. Don't worry about how it looks, just follow the illustration and then cut on the white line. Make a large neck opening, as shown.

2. With the white crayon, sketch the outline of the bat mask onto the black construction paper. Cut it out. Make a hole on each side of the mask for the strings. Tie a string to each side. Cut out holes for eyes.★

Monster Mash Cookies

Here's a monster-sized recipe for some Monster Mash Cookies. They are great to make for a Halloween party, for hungry trick-or-treaters, or to take to school.

INGREDIENTS★

1 cup sweet butter, softened
1½ pounds peanut butter
1 pound light brown sugar
2 cups granulated sugar
1 tablespoon light corn syrup
2 teaspoons vanilla
4 teaspoons baking soda
6 large eggs
1 cup peanuts
1½ pounds semisweet chocolate pieces
9 cups rolled oats (instant oatmeal)

UTENSILS★

measuring cups and spoons
large mixing bowl
mixing spoon
small mixing bowl
fork, 2 tablespoons
baking sheets, covered in aluminum foil
pot holders

HERE'S HOW TO DO IT★

1. **Ask an adult to help you turn on the oven.** Preheat the oven to 350° F.

2. In the large mixing bowl, stir the butter and peanut butter together. Add the light brown sugar, granulated sugar, corn syrup, vanilla, and the baking soda.

3. Break all the eggs into the small mixing bowl and beat them with the fork until they are light and lemon-colored. Now add them to the dough in the large mixing bowl. Mix well.

4. Mix the peanuts, chocolate pieces, and rolled oats into the dough. The dough will be very stiff so you will have to finish mixing it with your hands. (Of course you washed your hands before you started this recipe.)

5. Drop heaping tablespoons of the mixture onto the baking sheets, about 2″ apart. Bake for 10 minutes and, using pot holders, remove from the oven. The cookies will be soft when they first come out. Makes about 40 to 50 monster-sized cookies.★

Devil's Hot Fudge Sauce

This thick, rich chocolate fudge sauce is good enough to tempt the devil. Serve this sauce over a scoop of vanilla ice cream.

INGREDIENTS★

1/2 cup heavy cream
1/3 cup water
16-ounce package of semisweet
    chocolate chips

UTENSILS★

saucepan
measuring cup
mixing spoon

HERE'S HOW TO DO IT★

1. Ask an adult to help you turn on the stove and to cook the sauce.

2. In the saucepan, bring the cream and water to a boil. Add the chocolate chips and stir over a very low flame until the chocolate is melted.

3. Serve warm over vanilla ice cream. Store in a jar in the refrigerator. Leftovers can be reheated. Serves 6.★

Crackly Chocolate Cookies

The confectioners' sugar mixed into the chocolate cookie dough makes an interesting crackly design in these delicious little cookie treats.

INGREDIENTS★

4 ounces unsweetened chocolate
$\frac{1}{2}$ cup vegetable oil
2 cups granulated sugar
4 large eggs
2 teaspoons vanilla
2 cups all-purpose flour
$\frac{1}{2}$ teaspoon salt
1 teaspoon cinnamon
2 teaspoons baking powder
1 cup confectioners' sugar

UTENSILS★

measuring cups and spoons
medium saucepan
small saucepan
mixing spoon
large mixing bowl
small mixing bowl
plastic wrap
cookie sheets covered with aluminum foil
pot holders

HERE'S HOW TO DO IT★

1. **Ask an adult to help you turn on the oven and to use the stove.** Preheat the oven to 350°.

2. Fill the medium saucepan halfway with water. Place the small saucepan in it. Put the chocolate in the small saucepan. Place this on the stove, over medium high heat. Bring the water to a boil, then lower the heat so that the water is just boiling. Stir the chocolate until it melts. Be careful not to allow the boiling water to spill over into the chocolate. Set aside.

3. In the large mixing bowl mix the melted chocolate, oil, and granulated sugar. Add the eggs and vanilla. Stir until completely combined.

4. Now add the flour, salt, cinnamon, and baking powder. Mix well. Place the dough on a piece of plastic wrap, wrap it tightly, and chill overnight in the refrigerator.

5. Drop teaspoonfuls of the chilled dough into the confectioners' sugar in the small mixing bowl. Place the balls about two inches apart on the baking sheets. Bake for 10 to 12 minutes. This makes about 60 cookies.★

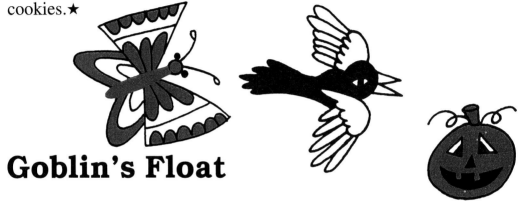

Goblin's Float

Here's a recipe for a drink that will cool you down fast, complete with a cherry on top.

INGREDIENTS★

1-liter bottle of ginger ale
1 pint vanilla ice cream
6 Maraschino cherries

UTENSILS★

6 tall glasses
6 teaspoons
ice cream scoop, or large spoon

HERE'S HOW TO DO IT★

1. Pour the ginger ale into the 6 glasses, but fill them only halfway up. Add a scoop of vanilla ice cream to each glass and top with a cherry. A jack-o'-lantern cookie would be great with this. Serves 6.★

Witches' Brew

Apple juice mixed with cherry juice, sliced banana, coconut flakes, orange slices, miniature marshmallows, and dusted with cinnamon is just the right refreshment for a Halloween night.

INGREDIENTS★

1-quart bottle of apple juice
12 Maraschino cherries
3 tablespoons Maraschino cherry juice
1 banana, peeled and sliced
2 tablespoons coconut flakes
1 orange, sliced
1 cup miniature marshmallows
cinnamon

UTENSILS★

measuring cups and spoons
large pitcher, 1½ quart
mixing spoon
6 tall drinking glasses

HERE'S HOW TO DO IT★

1. Fill the pitcher up to about 3″ from the top with apple juice. Now add the Maraschino cherries, cherry juice, banana, coconut flakes, orange slices, and marshmallows. Stir gently.

2. Pour the brew into the tall glasses, making sure that everyone has some of all the ingredients. Shake a little cinnamon on top of the brew. Serves 6.★

Crunchy Cereal Candy

Wrap up these candies in aluminum foil and give them to your friends on Halloween, or take some to school for a special treat.

INGREDIENTS★

1 tablespoon butter or margarine, to grease the pan
2 cups maple syrup
2 cups sugar
2 pounds semisweet chocolate chips
2 cups peanut butter
½ cup salted peanuts
10 cups raisin bran or other cereal

UTENSILS★

measuring cups and spoons
baking pan, 13″ × 9″
saucepan
large mixing bowl

HERE'S HOW TO DO IT★

1. Grease the baking pan and set aside.

2. **Ask an adult to help you turn on the stove and to use it.** In the saucepan, bring the maple syrup and sugar to a boil. Remove from the heat, add the chocolate chips, and stir until they are completely melted. Now add the peanut butter and peanuts. Mix well.

3. Put the cereal into the large mixing bowl. Pour the chocolate mixture over the cereal and stir until completely combined. Place the mixture in the baking pan and cut into pieces. Place in the refrigerator for about an hour until it is set. Makes about 50 pieces.★

Jack-O'-Lantern Cookies

Here's a recipe for an orange frosting you can use on store-bought vanilla sugar cookies or thin chocolate wafer cookies. Then make faces on them with raisins or chocolate chips. This is a good school project, or it might be fun at a Halloween party. Have the cookies ready on a platter, next to bowls of the icing and the raisins or chocolate chips.

INGREDIENTS★

2 cups confectioners' sugar
1/4 cup sweet butter, softened
3 tablespoons orange juice
3 drops of orange food coloring (optional)
1 box of vanilla sugar cookies or thin
    chocolate wafers
raisins or chocolate chips

UTENSILS★

measuring cups and spoons
mixing bowl
mixing spoon
table knife

HERE'S HOW TO DO IT★

1. In the mixing bowl, mix together the confectioners' sugar, butter, orange juice, and food coloring.

2. Using the knife, spread a thin coating of frosting on the cookies. With raisins or chocolate chips, make a face on each one, as shown. Makes 1½ cups of frosting.★

Index